FIND -A- WAY

WHAT I WISH I'D KNOWN WHEN I BECAME A HEAD FOOTBALL COACH

BY: KENNY SIMPSON

ACKNOWLEDGEMENTS

To write a book was something I had always hoped to be able to accomplish. To make this happen, I leaned heavily on several people that I admire and hold in deep respect. Many of them are people I view as mentors in the professional world and in my own personal world. I also had the help of three special ladies in my life that did everything in their power to help me edit and create a book that was something I hope to share with the coaching community.

My wife, Jamey Simpson, spends countless hours making me look good in every part of our life. This book is no different as she created the cover and helped with the title and editing. My mother, Kathy Simpson, is another special lady in my life and has always been one of my best encouragers. Finally, Kay Jones, my mother-in-law, took the time to painstakingly edit this book and helped in many ways with her encouraging words.

CONTENTS

Introduction

My name is Kenny Simpson and I have a love...make that an addiction, for building football programs from non-competitive to winners. Maybe it has been my love of the underdog. Maybe it's been my love of coming into a place that has low expectations and teaching a program to expect greatness. Perhaps it is because I enjoy surprising people. Whatever the reason (and I think it is some of all three), I have started my coaching career as a "fix-it" type coach.

I was born the oldest of five to a military family that moved about as often as most people change clothes. I was at three different high schools (playing football at two of them) from the 10th-12th grades alone. Even at a young age I loved the coaching aspect of the game. I never was satisfied to know just what we were doing, but always wanted to know why. This has led me to now have coached at three different schools in my 17 years of coaching. Each school had struggled in football before my arrival (although at first I was just an assistant coach) and each I was able to see become a competitive team in one year.

In this book you will read about the ways I have had success building programs that were not very competitive (one 8-23 previous three years and the other 2-28 with a 23-game losing streak) into competitive teams. I am not a miracle worker and many of the parts to this book will be things many of you already know, but maybe one or two of the ideas I have used can help you on your journey as a coach. Each chapter discusses different elements of becoming a successful head coach with a focus on turning around downtrodden programs.

Before I begin with football theory, I have to say this; you must love being a coach in order to have any success at any level. This sounds simple enough, but I have been around enough to see guys that may like what they do, but they love hunting, golfing or you name it and they are not willing to put in all the hours I think it takes to be a great coach. Don't get me wrong, I feel there are things in my life more important than football, however when people ask me for my hobby often times I tell them it is football. In my "off" time I read about football, study the game, study the great coaches and brainstorm about what I am going to do to be a better coach to my players.

I spend time with my family and love being around them. I spend time in my local church and put a lot of effort into it as well. You can do all those things even better than most people, because you don't have a job; you do what you love. My job is what I'd do for free even if I had to work somewhere else and just volunteer on the side. If you don't feel that way about coaching football, my recommendation would be to stop reading and start looking for what you should be doing with your life.

Love for your players must be at the top of the reasons why you coach. I have been around a lot of really great coaches that were very different in philosophies from offense to defense to how to run a practice, but each great one loved the kids. The coaches I have been around that I felt were not as strong or even weaker ones seemed to have lost or never really had a love for the players they coached. Most coaches care about their players, but do you care about them more than you do yourself. You have to be willing to make a decision that may cost "you" a win by disciplining a player to teach them. You have to be willing to be a mentor to players even after you may have dismissed them from your team.

There are tough parts about becoming very close to your team, the main one being the pain it will cause you personally if you have to let one go. Each player I have had to put off my team has caused me sleepless nights. It has driven me at times to tears. I have never regretted my decision, because if they get to that point with me they have definitely earned it, but I hurt for the fact that I will not be able to influence them as much. If you do not care for your players that much, I would say you are doing them a disservice and you may need to rethink your position as their biggest influence, other than their parents in some cases.

There are also many times that I am amazed by the greatness of the young men I coach. A few seasons ago we had just experienced what was, at the time, our biggest win in program history. After celebrating with the team and doing my normal post-game routine, I was getting ready to lock up and head out for the night still on a high from our win. As I walked by the locker room I heard our starting QB in the locker room so I ducked my head in quietly. He was in his locker next to a sophomore that was obviously very emotional about some family issue. I could hear the QB and still remember to this day how he was quoting scripture to the young man and encouraging him. Wins on the field are great things as coaches and we put a ton of time into accomplishing those, but I was a winner that night getting to witness a 17-year old understand what was really important.

One of the things we do in our program is a Father-Son Retreat. One of my former coaches, Ronnie Peacock, started this program and I thought It was such a great idea. I was very nervous about starting this event and it has, as expected, led to several very uncomfortable conversations with players. It has always amazed me how some of our players behave as well as they do with zero guidance from home. We have several wonderful fathers, but we have many more that succeed even though their home life is in shambles. We have our assistant coaches fill the role of "father" for several of these boys who have no one to attend. Talk about giving perspective to your coaching staff. Our younger generations are losing what a father used to be — someone that was consistent with love and discipline, who taught us how to persevere through tough times. If you get nothing else from this book, please consider doing this in your program, it may be the best thing we do in ours. This is his website with more information: **https://www.legacy.com/**

This book is geared towards coaches taking over struggling programs. Although, like all books, it will also deal with many of the issues that all coaches deal with. Take whatever you can use and ignore the rest. I don't pretend to know anywhere near enough to claim to have even most answers. I am just telling what I have learned in my years of coaching football.

FIND A WAY

Getting the Job

The Interview:

Before I even begin giving tips on what I did in my interview let me lay the groundwork you must do to get the opportunity to interview. Very often jobs that have not been successful are not too difficult to get interviews for if you have some experience and follow a few simple rules.

#1: Find someone that knows someone where you want to go. I attempted to land several jobs at an equal or even lesser level than the ones I finally came away with that I could not even get an interview. Many jobs have 100's of applicants for the job you want. The best way to get to the interview room is to work the phones with friends and friends of friends until you find the connection. This sounds simple, but it is always the best way to assure yourself of an interview. If you work hard enough you can find a connection.

#2: A solid resume. There are hundreds of ways to do this, but you must have a resume that makes you look different. It has to be true, but find ways to show what you have done and how successful you have been. There are a number of great resources and people that can help you with your resume and I would recommend updating it each year whether or not you are looking for a new job. When it comes to social media outlets, be very conscientious about what you post. Many places are going to consider that part of your digital resume.

#3: References. These must be strong people that will be known to the school you are applying, but need to be people that actually know you well. Using former employers is a must when applying for other jobs, but be careful as I learned the hard way, and understand that your current employers may not really like to know you have applied elsewhere. You may also want to have 7-8 people that you can use and tailor your resume for a specific job. For example: if you are looking at a job in a specific area of the state, you may want to use references that know the superintendent or may know someone in that area. It is all about connections and the more you can make, the better your odds of landing a good job.

There are 100's of ways to coach a team and be successful at it, from Dick Vermeil's tears and emotion to Nick Saban's glare, but the biggest problem many face is we don't know how to sell ourselves. Most coaches were not trained on interviewing for a very political position (which a head football coach is) and so many go into interviews unprepared for what can be a grueling interview. I will give you some tips that I experienced in my interviews, but the best way to prepare for an interview is to study up on the people that will be doing the interview.

Know something about the superintendent and principal and athletic director if possible. Knowledge about where they went to school or some other type of connection can make you stand out in the interview. Usually this information is easily accessible by looking at the school's website. This is a small thing, but most will like the fact that you spent time researching them.

There are several websites that can give you the pretty standard questions (what is your strength? Weakness? What makes you different?). All of these are good sites and you need to have a very good idea what you will say to these questions. Do the best you can to prepare for the expected questions, but be aware you will generally get several questions you were not expecting. It is ok to take time to find an answer (I usually repeat the question or ask for clarification to buy time if I need it), but it is not ok to have no answer for a question.

I have gone into each interview I have been able to gain for whatever position with the mindset of being myself. You obviously want to impress the interviewers, but I don't want to gain a position with them thinking I am someone I am not. You also want to find out as much about the school as possible. I have always written out questions I wanted to know. These typically dealt with off-season program, budget, coaching hires/moves and other areas. I learned quickly to also ask about when they expected to make a decision, as it gave me an excuse to call if I had not heard anything (also it is usually not a good sign if that date passes and they have not called, just a head's up).

One small thing I have learned is to also send a thank you card or email (I prefer the card) to the interviewers thanking them for the opportunity. Again, you are trying to set yourself apart from all other contenders for the position and this lets the school know you are someone that goes above and beyond. You will want to mail this to them the day of, or the day after your interview to be sure it gets to them quickly.

I have been in several head coaching interviews so far and each were vastly different with one giant exception, NO ONE IN THE ROOM KNEW MUCH ABOUT FOOTBALL. The questions had nothing to do with x's and o's or if I even knew the general rules about football. I learned then and there that getting a head coaching job had a lot more to do with how you could sell yourself and the program you were going to bring to the job. On a side note if they are very concerned about the type of offense or defense you will run, that may be a red flag of another sort.

I am not saying do not bring playbooks, philosophies, and football related material. I am simply saying to not expect that to be a major part of the interview. Usually it will be touched on somewhat to discuss coaching needs (number of assistants, types of jobs each will have) and organizational (practice times and off-season), but that will not be the meat of the interview. At a few schools I was asked basic questions about the type of offense or defense I preferred and how I chose to run those, but I was not asked nearly as many X and O questions or philosophy of offense or defense as I was when I interviewed to become a coordinator.

Come prepared with some type of folder to hand out to everyone in the room. This should include: copy of resume, cover letter, powerpoint (printed) of your vision for a program, handouts over "off the field" activities and assistant coach/player development plans and anything else you wish to leave behind. Find someone that is good at making these look professional and make sure it is representing you well.

I am very blessed to have a wife who is an excellent graphic designer. Each year we have worked very hard to come up with a Media Guide that is as professional as most colleges. It takes more of my (and of course her) time than I'd like, but it is something that our community loves. It also plays very well in an interview when administration can see how you are promoting your program. I'd highly recommend finding someone with the skills to help you complete something along these lines.

Over my time as a coach I have also been able to speak and organize several clinics. I had our school's graphic designer (I didn't want to overuse my wife since she already does so much for me) come up with a basic background for my clinic sessions. I also use this background on anything I put together for an interview packet. My wife came up with a cover page for it and I use it on everything. The goal is simply to look professional. While none of this actually shows if I know football or not, it does show that I am aware of the image I am portraying to the public. If you are looking for a job, remember you are competing against other guys that know their stuff, so you must stand out.

What's unfortunate is that I know several coaches that would be great as a head coach, but seem to struggle with the actual interview. To me it comes down to a few very simple things:

Vision: Know what you are about and what you want to do. Again there are 100 different ways to be successful, but all of them start with a clear vision and knowing what you want to do and how you will accomplish it. Don't wait for this question as it may not come in the interview. Go into the room prepared with a powerpoint, or folder or handout that describes exactly what your vision and philosophy is. If the question is asked that is a great time to present. If you hand the materials to the interviewers early on that will guarantee a selling point and a chance for you to talk about what you will do at that program. Just be ready and prepared with details from offseason, community involvement, academics, discipline and how you will handle these.

Passion: Many times nerves play a huge role in an interview, but you must show you are passionate about what you do. I believe the reason we coach is because that is who we are not what we do and you must sell this to the school you are talking with. Hard work and love of your job cover a multitude of shortcomings you may have on your resume. Be sure to show the energy and love for your job in the interview. You want to slow down and be sure to not come across too eager, but you also need to show the passion you have.

Articulate: If you don't have a big vocabulary start now working on one. The people interviewing you have doctorates and masters and want a clearly educated man for this position. Be professional throughout. A larger vocabulary is a simple thing to help in any interview.

Another thing you need to do in any interview is to have items that are on your "must" list as a head coach. This may be different for you than it is for me. Find ways to ask these questions or get the answers by listening during the interview. To find a job you will be happy with, you need to have your "musts" as something the school says they will provide or allow you to build. Here is a sample of my list:

1. Opportunity to bring in coaches in the near future that align with my beliefs and the freedom to move any coach on staff to any position I feel necessary.

2. Year-round weight training and conditioning program for all athletes (especially those in spring sports).

3. Support from administration on my decisions for discipline and removing athletes from the team if I feel it necessary.

4. Commitment to upgrade facilities/uniforms/needed items in the near future.

5. Ability to raise my own money through a booster club if needed.

One question I am stealing from another coach --- "Coaches can win games, but administration helps win championships. What will the administration do to help our program become the best it can be?"

Your list may include all of these, some of these or none of these. But make sure you feel comfortable with your list and how the school feels about it. This may cost you some jobs or you may have to turn down some jobs that will not work with what you feel is needed, but my recommendation would be to steer clear of those jobs anyway. If you can get what you feel you must have for a successful program, your odds of finding a place you can attain success will go way up. If you settle for a job, be sure you are willing to live with what is promised.

Taking a job at a high school usually involves several reasons, but if you take a job that you have not found out the right information you need, you may be in over your head in a no-win program. Be sure to understand that there were reasons that a school has not been successful and learn about them. If you are comfortable after learning why they have not been a good program and feel you can bring a good change, then take the position. Picking the right job is important as a coach looking to turnaround a program, but knowing what job not to take is even more important.

I Got The Job...Now What?

The Program:

Selling your program is a must. This is what you have to offer a school. I have always felt there were 100's of different ways to be successful as long as you believed in what you were doing and are passionate about it. If you have not already done so, work on your coaching philosophy. Steal the great ideas you love that others have used and make your own program. Work details like style of offense/defense, parental involvement, how to manage the booster club, practice schedules, dealing with discipline/grades, etc. This will help you be ready for most situations before they occur and will help you in selling what you do to others.

Most of us when we take our first head coaching position know what we would like to accomplish, but I was amazed by all the little details that I was unprepared for. If you haven't already, sit down with a head coach that has been around for a long time and ask him about all the details he handles every day. I knew about X's and O's to a degree as a young head coach, but I had to learn on the fly with handling every other part of the program. If you know what you will do before a situation arises with discipline or with how to spend money (or make money) or how to deal with your booster club/cheerleaders/band you will be much better off.

Your program needs to be something that represents you. I borrowed from all the coaches I worked under (using the good, and making sure to put other items on my "never going to do this" list). Whatever you decide you need to be behind 100%. Better to fail with your beliefs and decisions than to be someone that is unsure of himself. (You will always fail if you are unsure).

As I have grown in experience as a head coach, I have learned that any area you do not address with your assistant coaches and players up front is sure to become something you will have to address later. You would think it would be a waste of time to mention being at practice after school is mandatory, since players/coaches should know this, but I have found it is better to state the obvious. Each year I hand out a coach's manual for my assistant coaches that we go over early in the spring. In it is the role of each coach and what is expected as well as a lock-up schedule. When I first started this manual it was 10 pages. It now numbers close to 100 as I learned you must go over details if you want your program to run smoothly. Here are a few of the items we address each year as a coaching staff and we go over with the players:

1. **Schedule and expectations** of when each practice will start. Arrival time for coaches and players.

     a. Inside our schedule we also include all meeting times for the entire season and offseason. I give these out very early in the year. We do make a note that the times may change if needed, but I do my best to get this in my assistant coaches hands. We also have a schedule we get to the parents as soon as we can with all times we will need their son.

2. **Dress during practices** (coaches and players), to and from games and during any football related gatherings. I have gone over this for players each year and usually you will get tested early with something subtle. Make it a big deal and punish it immediately as this will head off any other issues you have. You can tell the discipline this has instilled with my programs as I have become better at enforcing a dress code. It has also instilled pride in our athletes.

     a. We try to encourage dressing the same by getting 3-4 shirts each year for our players. We raise the money through the booster club for this. The boys look forward each year to a new shirt and it makes it much easier to demand them dress like a team.

3. **Lock-up for the season** (coaches). I usually rotate between coaches and include myself first on the list. I allow assistants to trade days, but they must work it out on their own. I will hold the person responsible on the list if it is not done that day. On a side note, I usually put the coaches that seem eager to leave on the list more often than the ones that I know work hard every day. It is a good way to assist in running off coaches that are not willing to do what it takes for the program.

4. **Rules and regulations** for players. This is whatever you want to make. This is usually my least detailed document and I cover major infractions and punishments. Be careful not to paint yourself in a corner and always list that dismissal from the team is an option depending on your decision.

5. **Roles of coaches** and players before and after games/practices. We have different areas as a staff, from meeting the opposing team or officials to bringing statistics to me or giving to the media. We also have coaches assigned to making sure the locker room (home or away) is in great condition. Collecting pylons, assisting in closing down pressbox, even bringing food to the coaches meeting area after the game are covered in this list. I could go on and on, but I have learned that if everyone knows what role they have early on it is much easier for you as a coach.

   b. Players: We usually rotate locker clean-up (sweep/mop) between the team. We also may have younger players' roles as to who is in charge of the kicking block or catches for the kickers on XP/FG or helps the managers get the water where it needs to go.

   c. Managers: We always do our best to take care of giving great recognition to our managers, because we work them very hard. Most student managers will do what you expect of them and it is important early on they understand they have several jobs to do. We assign many of our pre/post game set up or clean-up of the field to them.

Be ready to be questioned about what you are going to do, especially from the former staff if you keep any. And they deserve to know the reason behind what you are doing. Don't accept constant questioning, but be open with them behind closed doors. Successful staffs always have the motto that inside the doors we may fight, but when we go on the field, community, school or locker room we are all together. If you have someone on your staff that does not abide by this, I'd recommend cutting them loose, for "a house divided cannot stand".

I have been very blessed with some great men around me as assistant coaches. In those weekend meetings when everyone is exhausted I want guys to feel free to speak their opinions, and we have had some great "conversations" mainly about personnel and scheme. Once a decision is made I've always had a policy that we are all in agreement. Most of the time this is followed by my coaches. In the rare occasion it is not, I call the coach in and am very clear that we will all work together for our team, even if that means we don't take their suggestion.

One thing I have always done with coaches is given them a built in excuse to their significant other to blame me for all the time they must spend away from home. We will not sacrifice for the job and that means spending a lot of time working, but I don't want to see marriages and families split because of something I am doing. That also helps me to be mindful not to waste coaches' time. I have seen 3 potential solutions to not waste time:

1. Set a clear agenda for any meeting.
2. Any specific meeting for a coach or groups of coaches should be done before a group meeting.
3. Set up meeting during times that families would not be awake — one coach had 6am on Saturday so they could be done by noon and spend time with family.

Work With The Parents:
I am not a huge fan of parental involvement in any coaching aspect. Our rule is that parents are welcome to watch practice from outside the fence. However, selling your parents on your program is a must at most schools, especially those that have struggled for some time. They will be the ones that will help with raising money, work days, pep rallies and other things that need to be done to create excitement

for your program. This means you must be able to sell them on your program.

I am a huge believer in over-communication with parents (which will be a whole chapter later in this book). Email is a wonderful thing, and also social media if used correctly. There are very few excuses for coaches in today's world to not communicate with parents. Here are ways I have communicated with parents:

1. We have always had **2 parent meetings**, one in the spring and one in the early fall. In this meeting we cover necessary materials (rules, expectations of players). We also allow our trainer to speak to the parents about what we are doing for safety and what to do if there is an injury. We cover our emergency procedure in case worse comes to worst. I speak about what is important to me (helping boys grow into men, integrity and pride in our team, school and community). We allow our booster club president to speak about their needs. I make this meeting mandatory for my coaches (especially the first time you host a parent meeting), so they can also hear what is said to the parents and I can introduce them.

   We stress this meeting to our players throughout the offseason and let them know we will be taking up names of those in attendance. I have also heard of coaches feeding the parents as a way to get them to show up to these meetings. It is very important that your parents know what is expected of them and of their boys throughout the year. I'd recommend doing whatever is necessary to get them in the seats. This will not solve all your problems, but it will cut down significantly on parents using the "I didn't know" excuse when you have to discipline their son.

   I also collect parental email addresses from this meeting. This is my main way of communicating during the season. It is pretty simple to make a group contact on Microsoft Outlook that will serve you very well the rest of the season. I will go into detail on this in my next point, but I'd recommend for you to make sure to get any and all contact information on your parents and have them sign any travel sheets or other rules sheets you may need them to sign.

I go over as many items as I can think of that may become issues throughout the year: Missing practice, academic expectations, dealing with injuries and other sorts of items that parents should know ahead of time. The first year I coached I just said we will practice after school every day and that was all I gave them as to our practice schedule. After the first year I had kids tell me they had vacation on Labor Day and other teacher workdays and would miss practice. I learned quickly to go through each and every day and time you expect players at practice.

2. The second type of communication is **weekly emails**. I send these out Sunday night or Monday morning with several items included. We have the weekly schedule on each email. Also included is any email address from the booster club or information about pep rallies. This has helped me on many occasions as parents will be the ones giving rides to several of your younger players or arranging travel. I had always had a hard time disciplining a player for being late to practice in the summer, because the parents were the ones bringing them to practice, and if the time had to be moved or changed they had a reasonable excuse. By sending our schedule out 4-5 months ahead of time with practice times and having weekly emails that deal with any changes that have to be made, I now have no issue running a kid that is late or doesn't make arrangements ahead of time.

These emails also provide an avenue for you to go over all announcements with fund raising or game night information needed. I have usually also given our booster club president this list and let them use it for fundraising items. Also, be sure to include your superintendent and principals on this list. I was amazed at the thanks I received from them at how I was on top of things and organized. This also helps with any issue you may have with a parent complaining if the administration knows you have already handled and discussed rules and issues.

3. **Social Media** -- Find a way to make social media work for you. Form a Facebook group to put pictures, announcements and anything else to make your program look good. This is also another way to promote your program. As I have continued to age, I have found this duty to be more fitting of a younger assistant. While I am not exactly a fan of having to put everything on social media, it is the way the younger generation operates and they love to see it.

4. The final way I try to make sure I am communicating with parents is through two activities that I have stolen from other coaches. The first was a **Mom's Football 101** meeting. This typically takes about an hour and we go over equipment used for football players, basic rules of football and then we run them through some "drills". It is a great night for the moms (we offer to any mom 3rd-12th grade) and creates great communication for us to most moms. I'd highly recommend this to any coach as it is great PR for you and your staff. I was shocked at how many mothers we had show up the first time we did this and how many brought notebooks to take notes. They want to be involved and help their son and this is a great way to educate them. We also take this time to describe how we handle injury situations and tell them about the caution we are taking with their sons. This has helped on many occasions as they will now come to you with any questions instead of sending their son off to the dreaded family doctor (which for me has meant that the boy is down for 2-3 weeks with an ear infection or some sort of ridiculous reason).

We also have done a **Father-Son retreat** for a few years. This may be one of the best things I have done as a coach. It can create some tension for those players without fathers, but we use our assistant coaches or the players pick an uncle or another male role model to come be with them. The scary thought is some of these players will be fathers within 3-4 years or less and having a retreat where you discuss the importance of fatherhood is something our world needs a lot more of. We have brought a former coach of mine, Ronnie Peacock, in to do our father-son retreats and it is great for the boys, but really great for the fathers. This is a great chance to be around the boys and their fathers and let them know what you feel is really important. I was shocked with how many had strained relationships with their fathers and you could tell immediately this was a good thing for them. I have had many dads come by later and thank me for having this. Coach Peacock reads a quote from one of his fathers that says, "I have touched my son more today than I have since his birth". That sums it up for me, a chance for fathers to grow closer to their sons. If the world had more of this it would be a much better place for all of us.

A new event we have started doing is a **Mother-Son date night**. We have done plenty of different activities from paint parties, movie nights, etc… This has been one of the most successful events each year and has not been very difficult to organize. We have our players dress up, seat their mothers, get their food and anything you'd expect from a boy on a date.

You may have other ideas, but all these "outside" activities help with a few areas. The first is that they let the parents and athletes know you care about them as people and not just players. The second thing is it allows for you to see what players are dealing with in their home life. Many will have no one show up, and many that do come give you a good idea that the apple doesn't fall far from the tree. The final thing these do is bond your team and coaches as a football family. To me a team that feels that close will do anything necessary to be successful on the field and off the field.

When things get rough (and they will throughout a season) when "Johnny" isn't playing where or as often as he "should be", it is good for your parents to know you care about their son. As a coach, each player should be important to you, and this helps parents know you do want what is best for each player.

I have also worked to have several roles that parents can be a part of our program and we want/need them to fill for us. Usually if parents have roles they can sign up to be involved in, this will help as you will get the ones that actually want to work for their son. Here is a list of areas I use parents:

1. Chain Gang: I usually have a group of men that want to be close to the action and they love being our chain gang. We get them a polo for games and hat so they will look as professional as possible. I also work with the "head" of the chain gang to make sure each game is taken care of. Usually the same men will work as a crew, but I want to double check. We also talk about our philosophy on offense since we want to be a hurry-up team and go over that it is important for us to have the chains moving as quickly as possible.

2. Pre/Post game meals: I usually have a mom that will coordinate all of my pre/post game meals or snacks. This is a big job, so you need to be careful in who you pick. I am always very willing to meet with this person to help in any way possible. (We write thank you notes to all churches/businesses that donate or help and make sure any help we get is appreciated). Usually the person in charge will pick a group of moms and they handle much of this job. Be sure to get the moms shirts or some other token of appreciation, and I usually get something nicer for the mom who is heading up our meal program.

3. Work days: In the past I have tried to have at least 1 "work" day for parents in early August to take care of areas around the football facilities. Anything from fresh paint to edging areas around the field house is on our list to get accomplished in one big day. In the past I have seen these days tied in with an inter-squad scrimmage (although I have not tried that yet) or a big meal. This is a great way for parents that want to help out and be involved to be used in a way that benefits the program.

4. Touchdown (Booster) Club: This will usually be an issue you will need to run past your superintendent first, but I feel a good booster club is essential for a coach to be able to build up the football facilities. There are many different ways to run a booster club, but be sure you have control of what is going on with money raising and where money is spent. The best way to do this is to be involved with the leaders in the booster club if it is already in existence. If one has not been started, I'd highly recommend starting one. I have done about everything under the sun with the team to raise money, but it has always worked better when

the parents are involved, and the best way to coordinate that is through a booster club. This will also take some of the burden off of you as a coach if you have a group of parents that are assisting in raising money and keeping the facilities as nice as possible.

Working With The players:

Selling the players on your program may be one of the easier parts of selling your program. I have learned a few things in coaching and one good lesson is that players will believe in you if you can show them you have a vision, you care for them and you will push them to be the best they can be. I have typically used many visual aids around our field house with motivational slogans and always had whatever our theme for the year is posted for the players.

One thing about players that I have learned that is more difficult to sell them on is they see right through anyone that is not being honest with them. You can get players to believe in themselves, but you must be honest with where the team is (especially teams that have struggled) and set reasonable goals. Usually my first years at programs we set no goals on wins or losses. Instead we focus on off-season goals (like increasing their squat or power-clean), academics and other areas that players have complete control over. These are relatively easy to attain and will breed confidence. Meeting your team where they are and showing them how to succeed in areas they can control is the starting place to turning around their mindset.

Players also love structure and knowing what is expected. We post our workouts, practice schedules and conditioning schedules for them all to see. We also talk about what we are trying to get out of each session. I believe in not wasting time, and most players that I have coached are the same way. They want to know why we are doing what we are doing. You can force players to work hard, but I have found you will get more accomplished if they want to work toward a goal. If you can set up an atmosphere and mindset of working smart and hard, most players will respect you much more for it and be more likely to give great effort. Very few players go into a workout/practice/game wanting to be lazy. It is much more likely that programs that have not been successful are full of players that don't understand why you do certain drills, clean the locker room or stress academics. They are willing to work hard for you if you can show them the "why" to your program.

As I have gotten older in our profession, I've learned I spend more time with our assistant coaches teaching them what I value, than really our players. I'm still around the players, and value my time with them, but they tend to gravitate to the young assistant coaches. Embrace this change when it comes in your career, but be ready for it. Teach your younger coaches how to handle this. Empower them to lead these young men. Lift up and praise your assistant coaches publicly. They are often the first to be able to cut off potential problems or draw kids into your program.

Sharing the Vision

Each coach must come up with his own vision. Many are different and personal to the coach or team. In this chapter I will share my vision and why I decided on it. If you can use any part of this chapter, please feel free to steal it and use it. I made a decision a long time ago, and many of you may have as well, about what kind of coach you want to be. To me wins and losses are important (they are to every coach), but if I am not impacting the young men's lives that I interact with each day and making them better people, then I am not doing my job.

"To bring honor to our community, school and football program in every area". That's it for my vision. It is very broad on purpose and usually requires me explaining exactly what it means. While the main vision is broad and all-encompassing, I have several other goals that I go over with the team. (I will list those in the following paragraphs).

Having a relatively vague mission statement allows you as a coach much more freedom in punishment of those who are not living up to your goals. I have found in my short time as a coach to never paint yourself into a corner unless it is something you are completely sold on. So to that end I have very few rules, but each is enforced and known upfront. However, having this mission statement about bringing honor to our school allows me much more flexibility in dealing with the knuckleheads we all have in our programs.

A smaller goal we usually set as a team is to have each player on the team finish high school and give themselves the opportunity to do what they choose after school. This normally means having a high enough GPA and ACT to have the chance to further their education. I have coached in some different extremes. (One school 100% went on to college, and another, it was like pulling teeth to get them to want to finish. They were there for football and when that was done...so were they). This has to be adaptable to where you are, but the underlying premise is letting them know academics must be a priority. To make academics important to them I have had mandatory tutoring for those with below a 2.0 or an "F" in any class. This quickly gets those who are not really struggling, but being lazy in class in gear, and their grades typically go up quickly. It also allows me to know who is struggling and needs real help. I have found in most schools that teachers are willing to help kids if the boys will make the time to meet before or after school with them. We have used tutors after Thursday practice and Monday practices (usually our "short days"). One thing I have been careful not to do is have tutoring in place of another activity. (I don't want to "reward" kids going to tutoring by letting them out of practice, conditioning, lifting).

Another goal we have as a team is to out-work all our opponents. I know that every coach in the country makes that same statement. Our goal is not so much to out-work, although we do put them through some rough stuff, but to get them to THINK they are out-working everyone else. To "trim the fat" off the roster we have summer workouts from 6:15AM – 8:30AM Monday-Thursday. We put an emphasis on continual movement during the workouts. We have each lift starting on the whistle and do not have any dragging around. I will get more in detail about our weight program later in the book. We also run practice the same way. Reps, reps, reps. We will spend maybe 5 minutes of teaching time each day on the field (the rest is done before practice in meetings), and the rest of the hour each day is movement and reps. On an average day our receivers catch 200-300 footballs (almost all from one of our QB's). Our goal is to kill them in the drill work. Team then becomes conditioning. We will do conditioning in the summer, mainly for a mental thing (our practices give them enough already).

School pride is another goal I have as a coach. This usually means being involved with the band and cheerleaders to increase excitement. I am not a huge fan of pep rallies and "extra" stuff that takes focus away from the preparation for games, but when you are taking over a program that has suffered, you MUST create excitement among the players and your school. This is important for getting kids to come out for football in the future. I have done "movie night", black out pep rallies, organized car bashes, coaches vs seniors in volleyball and all kinds of crazy things to get the excitement level up at the school. It will ultimately come down to wins, but creating excitement among your players and school is the first step to ensuring you have every available athlete in the school wanting to play football. We have also worked heavily with the booster club. I have spoken at booster clubs, help start booster clubs and spent more time than I'll ever get back listening to people argue over shirt styles and fundraisers. This is something I feel every head coach, but especially one walking into a struggling program, needs to be a part of. Booster clubs have always been a great asset to me. I am big on my team looking the same and having nice attire to wear at practice and around school. They are walking billboards for your program, so you need to be able to find the money to give them nice shirts/sweats/shorts. This sounds almost like it is something silly, but I believe I have had kids actually come out for my sport because they notice all the nice stuff the kids get and how they view our program as one that cares about the athletes.

Discipline is a big part of football and will kill a program if it is not strictly enforced, especially at schools that may have issues with it on a large scale. I have been very fortunate in my career that I have served at 3 schools that have always had discipline issues, but my day is not completely covered from one discipline issue to another (I have heard horror stories from several of my coaching buddies in "rough" schools). I have found the general rule of thumb from older teachers/coaches that you need to come in much stricter early in your tenure as a head coach is correct. As a head coach, never sacrifice discipline for a chance to win a game. (I know it sounds cliché, but you will always have a hard time winning with discipline problems and generally you will have greater success with kids that buy in 100%).

Grow Your Program

Going into a program, especially one that hasn't won many games, it is important to make decisions in several areas that you have control over. You don't have much control over some circumstances (such as: strength of opponents, talent level on your team, etc...), but you must make wise choices in areas that you can control.

My Superintendent shared the following story with a group at a meeting and it has stuck with me:

"A man took a job at a company and worked hard every day. He was always on time and was willing to do all that was asked of him. Five-years down the road a promotion opportunity became available. The man applied for the job and did not get it. He was beaten out by a person that had been on the job for 6-months. The man was furious and demanded to see the boss that next day. The boss obliged, but asked the man to do one thing that day — go buy oranges for him.

The next day the man came in and dropped the sack of oranges he got and wanted to discuss the job. The boss opened with asking him what oranges he got at the store. The man grumbled that he wasn't sure and gave the boss back his change. Before moving on in conversation the boss called in the man who he had promoted.

The man entered the room and was asked by the boss if he got his oranges. The employee responded he had taken care of the need. He said he was unsure what the oranges were for, so he asked the secretary, and she told him it was for his boss's wife's birthday punch. He then called the wife to see if she had a preference and how large her party would be. Getting her answer, he knew he needed a large quantity of very specific oranges. He purchased the oranges, ran them by to the wife and let the boss know he had it taken care of. The other employee left the room with the answer he had been searching for."

Just because you have guys with experience on your staff, don't feel obliged to reward guys that are there. Look for guys that understand that just being in a position as a coach, doesn't make you a coach. Find men that understand the great responsibility they have been blessed to have. Keep all those men or find some. If you want to succeed as a coach, you must have people around you that care nearly as much as you do.

The first thing a coach must assess is the attitude of those on his staff, if he inherited them, and his senior class. You must teach and stress that you expect high energy and no excuses. Many times these people have been through a rough spell and are simply reflecting the culture around them. I've always looked for great attitudes and hard work as the two main characteristics I hire or keep in assistant coaches. If someone has these, I feel we can compete even if their knowledge of the game is lacking. The same applies in your senior class. Get rid of energy vampires, and don't allow them to suck the life out of everything you build.

When I'm given the chance to speak with a coach taking over a program that has struggled for years, I tell him the story of the frog. If you take several frogs and throw them into a pot of boiling water, most will jump out, but you still will boil several. However, if you put them all into a pot of cool water and slowly turn up the heat, they will all stay in the pot and boil to death. I'm unsure of your situation, but both paths work. If you are at a small school, and plan to be there for a while, I'd go with the slow cooker. If you are trying to get the staff you want, you may turn up the fire on your coaches and see who can make it.

I have listed and will talk about several in this book, but in this chapter I want to focus on a few simple things you can do as a coach early on to give your program the best chance to be successful.

Step one is a simple one to me, although some coaches may not agree with it. Schedule winnable games early in the year. As your program will grow each year, this is not something I'd recommend you do over a 10-year period, but early on as you are teaching your players to be successful, you should do your best to give them games they have a great opportunity to win. Most states allow coaches to schedule between 3-5 games and I'd pick those games wisely. This is especially true if your conference is a very tough one. For example: at my most recent school we played 7 games in conference and of the 7 games, 5 were teams ranked in the top 20 in the state. To help my team, I scheduled 3 winnable games early in the year. We started 2-0-1 and it helped the confidence of the team as opposed to playing 3 very tough games and being 1-2 or worse.

The next step for your program is more of a long term help. Start or become very involved in your feeder program. Most places now have football at the elementary level. It is a great step forward for your program to have your athletes play football from the 3rd grade on up. Many coaches "put-up" with this program or ignore it completely. At one school I was in, we actually made the program pay to use the field! These will be your players in 6-8 years if things go well.

Youth Football -- What I have done:

At one school, I actually held a coaching clinic for the volunteer helpers. We kept it very elementary in knowledge (going over safety precautions, practice scheduling, goals of the program) with very little x and o talk. I also gave out my cell number to the coaches on the team and invited them to be on our sideline for our "elementary night" game. I made it a point to attend as many home games they played and be seen by the sideline. This helped us draw kids in from our area, and we even had kids drive in from surrounding areas to be a part of our elementary program.

I have also worked each year to run an elementary camp. I usually have my varsity players help run the camp. We do a simple 3- day camp and charge a minimal cost (which is also a nice benefit for a young coach). I have always had many of the younger kids attend this camp, and they have a great time and feel involved in our program. It is also a great community event for your varsity players as many of them do very well in helping with the camp.

I could list story after story of some crazy situations I've dealt with in youth football from players to parents, but the reality is, if you are at a smaller district, you better be involved. I know the name of many of the young men that will be in our program, and I make sure they know who I am and what I stand for. I've found it much, much easier to get a boy out for football in the 4th grade than to talk a 10th grader or even an 8th grader onto the field. Like it or not many kids "specialize" (a word I hate) before even reaching junior high.

The final step I will go over in this chapter that you can do for your program is one simple word: Simplify. At most programs I have become involved with, the athletes were so confused about what was going on with the offense or defense that they had a hard time playing the game with speed. Be sure to teach the basics over and over again. This is important for any program, but it is especially important for a program that has struggled. We all know football is a pretty simple game. However, as a coach, one of the biggest mistakes I have seen from programs I have taken over is the previous staff had confused the players by doing way too much or not teaching each step of what they were trying to do.

My first practices with teams (usually in the spring) have been about teaching 1-2 concepts. We usually run 4-5 drills, but run them at a good speed and maximum intensity. I demand perfection from the players on whatever we are doing. (Usually we do tackling for ½ the practice). I explain upfront to the players and coaches that our goal is to be more physical and to become better at the fundamentals and that we will do certain drills to insure this happens. Most teams that are not very good at football are either not physical or not very fundamentally sound. It doesn't matter what offense or defense they run, if they aren't willing to be physical or are unsound in what they do, they will not win. Make sure you send this message loud and clear the first few days you are running the show.

Keeping the basics of football as your focus sounds like a simple thing to do, but it will be challenging for you if you are like me, as I want to put everything I have in and then figure out what will work. Don't move on from a concept offensively or defensively until you are completely satisfied with how well your team knows it. Many times we will only have 3-4 runs we will run all year the first season, but we will be perfect at what we are doing. Older coaches warned me, and they were correct, that you need to spend more time teaching how to block, run, throw and catch than you do putting in new plays. Defensively I have seen several defenses that run 20 different fronts, but have no clue about the concepts of any of them. Be sure that not only you know the concepts, but each of your assistant coaches and all of the players know what they are to do and why they are doing it. Stress playing hard and giving maximum effort over mixing up coverages and fronts. As a coach, it is much easier to put in new coverages or fronts once the defense has mastered your base look.

This book is not about X's and O's, but the most creative coaches I've seen spend time working on the fundamentals to the point their players understand them and why they are important. At that point they begin to show them different concepts. RPO world is a great example. Teach a base run and some screen concepts and boom you have 15 "plays". Or defensively teach how to blitz and roll coverage and you can have 20 fronts with kids doing it well.

Decide, Delegate and Depart

My father is a retired Air Force Colonel and has shared several pearls of wisdom from his time in the service. One that I will always remember is the 3 D's to leadership (although it may have been meant as a joke): **Decide, Delegate and Depart**.

As a self-proclaimed micro-manager I had no idea how to do any of this at the age of 28 (my first head coaching job). Instead I worked myself to death and became so upset that no one would help me. I had not learned how to communicate to those willing to help what I needed help with, or how to teach them the way I wanted things done. This takes patience and over-communication on the part of great head coaches. Your best helpers are the assistant coaches and next should be community people that want to help. I'm good at many things, but I know lots of people that have great skills. Learn how to use those people and follow the **3 D's**:

1) Decide on a plan of action
2) Delegate to a great person that can do that
3) Depart and let them take the issue and fix it.

Coaches will take ownership if you recognize their talent and allow them to have some leadership. When you do everything by yourself, you cannot get angry that others don't help. They can't read your mind!

Most coaches that have been around know that in order for a football team to be successful at the level most programs strive to be, there must be great support from many people. This can range from assistant coaches, administrators, booster clubs, parents, players, community, cheerleaders, band and students/teachers from the school. In some situations, most of this has already been set up. But I have found that at many schools that have not been successful, this is often a very overlooked area in the program. It is easy to see why. No coach likes handling most of the "other stuff" that comes along with being a head football coach. In a perfect job a coach handles football only and has no worries about facilities, raising money, doing interviews and speeches, working with the booster club, pep rallies, concession stand, pre/post game routines and helping players be recruited to college. However, this is the real world, and for those of you who have not been a head coach, get ready it is more than you imagined.

This to me is what much of my time as a head coach is spent on. Things that ultimately have nothing to do with X's and O's or player development. I have also learned that every little thing you can do that is unique and makes your players/parents feel special, will help you "recruit" legally, as athletes will want to be part of your program. To run a program the way I feel it needs to be will involve so much "stuff" you will have to be able to find people you trust and are willing to work. This chapter will show all the areas I have felt we needed to address, and the different ways I have addressed them. You may be in another situation, but we all know people that are either on our staff or good to the school to use in different areas. If you have been or are now in a smaller school like I am, you also know much of this will fall to you and, unless you have a plan, much of the little things will never be done.

Facilities:

Most coaches recognize this as an important part of the job. This is the biggest recruiting tool you have to any kids inside your school, or potential students, to your program. I have played terrible teams with great facilities and I have played great teams with terrible facilities, but usually teams that have great facilities will be the type of team that will maximize their ability. I think this is because someone, usually the head coach, takes pride in the program and wants the athletes to have the best facilities they can afford.

Most coaches learn very quickly that unless you are at a very large school, or one with a great tradition, taking care of the field, field house, weight room and other areas will all fall to you. Learn to delegate. Most coaches are hard workers by nature, but I have learned this may be one of the most time consuming areas of the job, and will definitely take a lot of time away from your family if you are not careful.

What I have done:

Worked with the dad's to form a great "paint crew". This is an easy way to let dads of your players be involved in your program. Usually the atmosphere is light and great to have dads and coaches work together to paint the field. We usually make a night of it the first time the field is done. After it has been painted the first time, we usually hand it off to the crew of dads, if you are able to trust them to get it done correctly. Your assistant coaches will love you for getting them out of this job. I have been very careful to make sure these dads are taken care of with our football program's apparel for all their help. Usually a hat and shirt will go a long way for most dads!

I have also assigned locker room clean-up to one coach that will answer to me. He gets with me as to exactly how I want each locker to look and what is acceptable as to cleanliness. We spend one afternoon showing the players what needs to be done. (It is good for them to see the head coach being involved in this also). In turn, he usually assigns clean-up by the week to the players with captains that answer to him. This sounds simple and many of you may already be doing this, but it takes the burden of any cleaning and puts it back on the players. We usually have to run 1-2 times early in the offseason in the first year or two that I have been at a school. If you run them hard enough they will only need to be reminded of what will happen should they not do their job. This is a perfect job for a younger coach or one that has a lot of fire still in the tank.

Field duty is usually one that I have not had as much control as to who gets assigned to it. Many times at a smaller school it will be you and another coach or two. If possible, try to do most of the field cutting/edging during the day. For example: When the team is getting a lift or watching film, I have let an assistant slip out and work on the field for an hour. That is a small thing, but with all the time coaches use already, any extra is appreciated.

Improving facilities is an important part of any program. As a coach, I usually go in with a list of improvements and a "dream" list as to what would make the facilities perfect. At one school, we were able to get: Fieldturf, a new field house, new weight equipment, a new press box and new home bleachers all within the first 3 years I was on the job. Many times coaches would be surprised what can be done by having a plan. Whatever your situation is, make a list of improvements and rank them from most important to you to least. If you are able to use some of the advice I will give you in the next section of this chapter you will be able to raise money. Be sure to always look for improvements to your facilities.

At my current school we went from a grass field, very limited seating, no home side press box, an outdated scoreboard, a weight room in a condemned building to some of the best facilities in our state for our level of school. All of this was done with community money. Our administration allowed me to go and find the money. Every school wants nice "stuff", but many coaches simply don't want to go out and raise the money, since it is much easier to simply say, "the school won't provide the money".

The weight room must be a place that is special to your team. You must have pride in whatever your school can afford. At one place I was in we had an old elementary building that was a 20x60 with our racks and weights. Our bars were falling apart, we didn't have enough weights and what we had was not very good. Before I came this had caused a "who cares" attitude among our athletes in the weight room. They were not putting the weight equipment back, they tossed equipment around and were not taking care of what little they did have. Once we made it clear we would take care of any small piece of equipment we had (a few frozen pushups, laps on the track and squat jumps later) our players pride went up. Obviously that was one of my items on my list that we worked very hard to improve. We actually came in with some mirrors we had found and mounted them on the walls. At one school I spent 2 days with my staff (who hated me for 2 days) painting the walls just to make the place look a little nicer. I'd recommend you have a weight coach at your school if possible. At my most recent school, I spent the first 4-5 months teaching all the lifts and routines to my players and several coaches, and at the end of that time named the coach most-ready for the position as the "strength and conditioning coordinator".

Raising Money / Booster Club:

A hated word by many coaches is "boosters". These people at some places feel they should also adopt the name "assistant coach". However, for a program to generate the money it needs, you will need people from the community and the booster club to help. Making contacts in the community is also essential if you are in the role of raising money for your program (and what coach would say he doesn't want nicer facilities/equipment/uniforms).

What I have done:

At most schools there will already be some type of booster club in existence. I immediately reach out to whoever seems to be in charge and start working with them to get the booster club (or touchdown club or whatever the name is) to become a usable entity for me. This usually requires a few meetings to see what they have done and also letting them know what your goals/needs are for your football program.

I have always developed a 3-5 year plan for improvements we will need. This will deal with anything from facilities to equipment to uniforms to coaches gear. You will need to prioritize clearly to the booster club what you want to raise money for so you don't start getting items that were not high on your list. Most booster clubs will be much more willing to raise money if they know what the money is going towards. I have also made it a point to attend the booster meetings (especially early on) to meet and greet all the parents/boosters that are working hard for the school's program.

A few tips on raising money for coaches:

Big companies are where you go for "big" money. When we raised money for field turf we accepted anyone that wanted to give, but made it a point to go to banks and large companies as our main "targets" as donors. Using individuals or selling items may raise a couple thousand dollars and is great for smaller items, but it will wear down your players/parents and booster club for not as much money as you will need if you have a big ticket item.

Form a committee for any big fundraising outside of the booster club (or even in conjunction with the booster club). This helps spread out some of the work if you are working on a big project. In the committee have people you invite because of their connections to the community and people that may have expertise in what you are doing. When we were putting up a new field house I included a Masonry expert, builder and one of my parents that handled flooring. These guys were great at getting me information I'd need and all volunteered as much time and money as they could to help us complete the project. People are very willing to do anything for their children and want to help in roles they can.

Surround yourself with people that are good at raising money if that is not your strength. In some cases, you will have a coach on your staff that has a gift in making connections with the community and asking for money. I am not weak in that area, but it was even better for me to have a coach or two that have been great at working with me to visit with banks/businesses and making contacts.

Interviews / Speeches / Using the Media:

I have been at a few schools and noticed coaches face 1 of 2 problems. Either they are not getting enough coverage for their team and they are fighting to get more, or they get too much and are not prepared for how to handle the media.

Let's start with the first issue. Many coaches at smaller schools or schools in large cities have this issue. Getting attention for your program through the media is important. If you want kids that have any type of choice to want to be a part of your program you must be able to show your program as often as possible (in a positive light) through the media. While you can't control the media you can do some steps to help yourself be shown in a positive light.

The second issue can be more difficult. I have not had as much experience with over-exposure, but I have had to work with 2-3 different newspapers and tv stations. My one recommendation would be to attempt to always stay positive and be sure to organize your schedule so you can meet with them. I have found that when you form good relationships with the media they tend to "help you out", or make you look better than when you do not have a good relationship with them. The pen is mightier than the sword in some situations and anyway you can help yourself in the media would be a smart idea.

What I have done:

It may sound simple, but being pleasant to the reporters (newspaper and TV) is something I have worked hard to do. No coach likes answering questions after a loss, especially a tough loss, but it must be done. I have always done an end of the game interview for our local radio station, win or lose, and I make it a point to get up there after the game after addressing the team.

Be available to the media. I have always made sure if I couldn't meet with an interviewer I would make an appointment (usually you can set a weekly or daily time to talk with one) to meet with the media. It is important that you are able to have your voice heard through the press. I also assign a coach to have statistics ready for me before I will meet with the newspaper/tv to go over a game. I want to have everything they will need and be able to get as many kids' names out there as possible.

Contact the media and let them know as much as you can. I have invited the Newspaper/TV stations to many activities we do as a football program. From our "Night of Champions" (a weightlifting event) to our end of the year banquet, it is important that your program gets the coverage it deserves. Anytime you have a boy sign to play college football make it a big event (even if they are signing to a small school). Many times the media will not show up to smaller events, but I have been surprised with how many times they come and cover things that every coach does anyway. This is great exposure for your football program and parents and players appreciate it.

Pep rallies / Cheer / Band

Not a favorite of mine, or I'd assume most coaches. Again some of you may be in situations with traditions already in place and that is great. I have found that if you can make contact with the cheer sponsor and band director and start a good relationship it will benefit you and your program in the future. I don't have an exact way of doing things, but I have found if you can include the band (maybe fight song after game?) and the cheerleaders in your program, school spirit is boosted, and you will have even more support from your school.

What I have done:

I have met with the cheer sponsor before the season and worked include homecoming events, pep rallies and any before/after games events. I have also met with the band director usually about practice schedules (if we share the field) and pre-post game routines.

I have also made sure we invited the cheerleaders to our end of the year banquet. We have also included, when possible, the cheerleaders and band in the senior night at our school. It is a pretty simple thing to do, and I have found the parents, sponsors and students have been very appreciative.

Concession stand / game management (off the field stuff)

As a head coach most of this stuff is the last thing you are concerned about. I have no clue what happens off the field on a Friday night during the game. What needs to be done with your administration and you is to walk through a typical Friday night and discuss where you need them stationed, where security needs to be and where emergency personnel needs to be also. We have worked all emergency situations (injury on field or bad weather) with the coaches and administration to make sure there will not be any questions if something were to happen.

I have often told my players and assistant coaches, "the difference between a boy and a man, is that a boy does what he wants to and a man does what he has to". This applies to all the off-the-field stuff that no coach enjoys dealing with. Those who succeed in our business understand that you must do these parts of the job well to be great as a head football coach. If you only want to do the "fun" parts of football, stay on as an assistant.

One thing I have not had to become very involved in was the concession stand. Most of the time this is already claimed by either the booster club or band or some other school entity. I would suggest if the profits are going to football in some way, that you be aware of what is being bought and sold. I have found that many times concession stands could be making much more money if they were running more efficiently. This again is something that can be done in the off-season, and usually delegated to someone else.

Helping players get recruited

This is a very under-rated part of coaching now. Every kid thinks they can play college football, and let me tell you a secret...if they are willing to go anywhere and have good grades there will be a college of some level willing to take them. Division 3 and NAIA schools are now "recruiting" athletes to play for them even on the JV level. This means many of these schools need to have 150 or so players to fund their program and they are looking for good students that want to play football. Many students love the idea of playing football, but would not make it in a college program, so you must weed out the ones that don't really want to play.

What I have done:

The first thing I do is find a younger coach and assign him the role of "recruiting coordinator" (not to get kids into our school, but to help them be recruited). This needs to be a coach that is great at making contacts and is willing to put in quite a bit of extra time.

I work with this coach to make a list of players that want to play college football. The first thing we do is look at academics. If the player has a high score on his ACT that is a great selling point for a lower level school. Most of these schools will stack scholarships, meaning they may get $2500 for ACT, $5500 for pell grant and $2000 for football. This allows a player to stack $10,000 towards their tuition and room/board. We talk about this with our kids from their 9th grade year on and many that have the goal to play college football understand how important this is.

The next part of our agenda is meeting with each player (we try to do this before his junior season if possible) and giving him our honest evaluation of where we feel he could play. We then have them make a top 10 list of schools. On this list they will include 2 "dream" schools, 5 "realistic" schools and 3 "last case scenario" schools. More often than not the "last case" schools are schools we have recommended. They do this list with the help of a parent and it should only include schools that: 1) Have their major, 2) They qualify for academically and 3) Are approved by their parents. From there we make a highlight video and call each school. Once contacted we send the film and inquire about camps (if the player is looking at a Division 1 or 2 school) the school may be hosting.

Involving your school counselor will take much of the academic part of the recruiting off of you. They are able to help the player (and we make the player do much of the work to see how serious they actually are about playing college football) walk through eligibility requirements for the NCAA and NAIA. Every dad feels their boy will play in the SEC or PAC-12, but the reality is many students can play at the division 3 or NAIA level and have a great time if they love football.

We cannot guarantee anything to a player, but typically if they have good grades (3.0 or above), work hard and score well on their ACT we can find a school that would be willing to give them some type of monetary package to help with their school. This allows many of your players the opportunity to continue playing football at the collegiate level.

There Is No Off-Season

I am going to fill this chapter with some pretty basic information about weightlifting since there are many people more qualified than me to bring this information to light. What I want to focus on is the fact that you must "win" in the offseason as a head football coach. This is the one time in the year that each team can achieve success. During the season it is pretty clear what happens each Friday night, but during the offseason each team can win.

Science and weight lifting have come a long way in just my short time as a coach. If you don't feel like reading the entire chapter, let me sum up what I feel about weight lifting programs: All of them (within reason) are great. That's it. I feel the weight program will be successful if your kids buy into whatever it is and put forth great effort. I have been able to meet with and watch several weight programs, and they all have slight differences, but each "successful" one has great energy by the coaches and players and they feel it is the best program in the state. I am not trying to knock any program or belittle different techniques of weight training. It is much like running an offense. They are all good if taught and run correctly.

Now there are several basics each coach needs to have in his program: Core lifts (Squat, Bench, Powerclean), and each needs a conditioning part as well. The key to a successful weight program is not so much what you are doing, but rather how hard you are working. This may sound as if I am dismissing the weight room experts, which is not at all the case. I feel there is a lot of value in looking at new and creative ways of strengthening your athletes, and as a Head Coach you need to be heavily involved in what is going on in your weight room. Each athlete needs to feel that the weight room is the 2ⁿᵈ most important part of your program. What happens on the field is more important than anything you can do in the weight room, so realize you need to make your weight room a tool to help with success on the field, not simply to see how much you can lift. We make weight lifting and conditioning a very high priority. I would recommend going to watch what other high school programs are doing that are successful or getting on the web and searching for programs.

The one thing I would say is to be careful not to completely copy a collegiate programs weight training. You are dealing with high school athletes and their bodies are not as ready for what the college programs put them through. You can work as hard as college athletes, but be careful not to run your athlete's bodies into the ground. I have been an assistant coach and watched our head coach run our players ragged early in the season until they had nothing left for the end of the year. There is a fine line between teaching your players work ethic and gaining a physical, tough mindset and wearing your kids down.

We also use our strength and conditioning program to help with other attributes I like to build in my team:

1. **Mental toughness**: This to me is more important than how strong or fast a kid is. I have learned that the "weight room warriors" do not always equate to the best football players. To that end we incorporate a lot of circuit type auxiliary lifts. The main purpose of these lifts (as well as hitting each muscle we are aiming to cover that day) is to have speed and wear the athlete down physically and mentally.

   We love to end most workouts with some type of simple mental toughness body weight type exercise. Anything from Core Bridges, Wall sits, frozen pushups, what we refer to as side planks (athlete is on elbow and only feet touch ground) can do what you are looking for. This is a great way to finish workouts as you watch the kids struggle with a simple task as they are already exhausted. It is also a way to see who will be mentally tough and who will lead when they feel terrible. Usually we will not allow the team to finish until all are "perfect" on whatever exercise we are doing.

One of the things I love to do starting out is "max effort" week on squats. The kids hate it, and you have to be careful not to use it too often, but it is great to start off whatever cycle you are using in your program. We have our boys do 55-60% of their max 30 times in the first set. The second set is 20 times, and the third set is at least 10. They have to get their reps or fail trying to do so. This is a great out of season workout and will really test them as it is an exhausting workout.

2. **Injury prevention**: All teams claim to have something they do that helps stop injuries. We have 3 parts to our program to deal with injuries. The first thing we do on each day, is to have a "injury prevention" lift. On Squat and Powerclean we focus on the legs (hamstrings) and lower back. "Good Mornings" are something we have used, as are Glute Ham Raises for the hamstring area. We have also gone with partner stretching on the hamstring and lower back. On bench day we do some type of shoulder lift (incline bench, chin ups with arms open to work shoulder, dumb bell work or "angles" as we call it). A lot of coaches have these lifts, we just make sure to get them in everyday.

The next part of injury prevention is our core work. Early in our offseason we will spend 10 minutes each workout (usually at the end) rolling through several core exercises with body weight with no rest (also a mental toughness exercise). We usually cut this down to 2 days a week later in the offseason and 1 day a week during the season. To make sure we continue to strengthen the core we have lifts in the weight room. I am a big fan of overhead squat (lower weight so the shoulders can handle it) as it is a total body lift. We also do "landmines" (putting weight on one side of the bar and standing bar on end as the athlete lifts from each side, almost in a swinging motion). We make sure to have 2 days of core lifts and 1-2 days of core with body weight each day in season.

The final part of our injury prevention is what our kids call our "yoga" day. Usually only done in the offseason as day 5 of the week (although we move it around to fit a day we want to use it). This day was laughed at until the boys experienced it. It has been great for core strength as well as balance and injury prevention. We do 35-minutes worth of your traditional "yoga" stretches. We originally viewed this as a rest day, until we saw the flexibility it gave many of our athletes. Now we use it every week as a normal workout.

3. **Discipline**: Every coach wants and needs discipline in his program. Whether you are coaching football or tennis each program needs to have athletes disciplined in their sport. I have found the best place to accomplish this is in the weight room and conditioning program. The weight room needs to be a place that lazier athletes dread going to each day. We want to create a workmanlike attitude from the minute a workout starts.

Usually we will give a 2-3 week learning period. We will get all our lifts in during this period, but are usually spending 15-20 minutes a day teaching the correct form or watching for it in all lifts. We will break apart tougher lifts (powerclean, clean and jerk, overhead squat) and teach them part by part. We will explain how and why we use each lift. During this period, you cannot let something move on until it is done the right way. Do not move to another lift until all your boys are doing exactly what you are asking. We point out that this is not just a safety precaution, but it is also a way to do the "little" things right.

The next phase of our program is the intense phase. We intentionally test kids on physical and mental ability by making our program move at a very fast pace. Usually we post each athletes max and percentages by their rack. We assign groups of 4 to each rack and spend a day going through routines on changing weight (starting with the lowest lifter and moving up, helping with math on what plates to use, who should spot and who is resting) to make sure we can move fast on our core lifts. We love circuits for our supplemental lifts and to hit areas of the body we feel are important. All of these pre-workout details being taken care of allows us to move very fast in all our lifts. We can usually get a "main" lift and all supplemental, injury prevention and core work take 40-50 minutes depending on the day.

The conditioning phase of our workout is as important mentally as the lifting. I am careful not to run them too much early on as we don't want some of our skill kids to run off the weight we are trying to put on. So we usually put them in groups (those maintaining or gaining weight in one group and those trying to lose weight in another). The ones that are maintaining work sprints only. All have to be timed to insure great effort. We range from 20 yard – 50 yard sprints and range the amount depending on the day and time of year. The ones that are trying to lose weight will do sprints (about ¾ the first group) and will do some type of middle distance running (from 6 ¼ mile sprints to a 2 mile run) to be run after the sprint work.

4. **Winning attitude**: The weight room is great, because any kid can win. The goal is simply to be better than you were before you started. We have made each kid's goals (reasonable) for them to shoot for at the end of a cycle. We tend to do 6-8 week cycles depending on the season. In a cycle we hit lower weight, 60-70% and high reps, early and go to heavy weight, 90-95% and low reps, late. Our kids usually improve each lift from 10-20lbs depending on the kid. We have had improvements much greater than that (actually more often than we would have thought) and sometimes have a kid that will gain less. The main thing is any kid willing to work in the weight room can feel like a winner. For teams that have not experienced winning on the field, this is a relatively easy way to start to change that culture. I know that every team (well almost every team) "wins" in the offseason, but we make this a big deal. I have ranged from a "Night of Champions" to a "Flex off" to actually winning a state championship with our powerlifting team.

When dealing with a team that has not had much success, a coach must find a way for the team to win at small levels. We have always started with testing in each area we feel important: Squat, Powerclean, Bench Press, 40 time, Pro-agility and several other jumps. The runs or tested categories could be anything. The idea is to make sure athletes see the improvement and the importance of being at each workout.

5. **Consistent Participation**: Many schools that were not successful do not have good attendance in the off-season program. This must be addressed and stressed, and I have seen the best way to do this without running kids off (that will happen to some anyway, but this may limit how many you lose) is to show them the purpose and improvements the team will make.

    I have also done shirts or other rewards for our athletes that do not miss a workout or miss less than 3 for the entire offseason. In most schools that have not been successful, it is not uncommon to have athletes deliberately missing days of their offseason. While punishment will also work, we like to reward our athletes that are doing things right. We have also given awards for top 5 for lifts or weight classes, biggest improvement and hardest worker. The idea is to have enough awards that any athlete can have an opportunity to win. Anyone can work hard and even your weakest players can win the improvement awards.
We also do our best to have "make-up days" on free days or team building days for the rest of the team. We build one in a week so that athletes that miss will make them up. We do not allow unexcused absences, but I have found it is very hard to fight an "illness" excuse from athletes and this seemed to help us stop having as many kids being "sick" on squat or conditioning day. If an athlete does not miss, they can use their make-up day, as a free day. We usually have 90% of ours that get one free day a week in which we do some type of team-building activity. (Usually we do something requiring a lot of movement, which actually gets quite a bit of conditioning) or install day (closer to the season).

During the summer we work-out Monday – Thursday and give our athletes Friday – Sunday off. This is a great day to use as a make-up day for those who miss. This is when we lose most of the players that are not with the program. We schedule workouts early in the morning (usually 6:15am). This is done for 3 main reasons: 1) We want to run off those not committed to the program by this point, 2) We want to ensure boys have no excuse to miss a workout, and this enables them the opportunity to work a job during the summer if they choose to. This also makes sure that parents that have to drive them to workouts are able to without work being an issue (our coaches will drive kids back home after workouts if need be), and 3) This helps us to run a full conditioning and install period outside with not too much heat (although in Alabama and Arkansas it may still be in the 90's at 8am).

There are a lot of different summer workouts and I know many of them work, but this is the one I use and would recommend.

This type of workout plan for the summer has several advantages from the coaching aspect also: 1) If you have a small staff, having one workout and conditioning/practice time makes it easier to have your entire staff there (and having it over by 8:30-9:00am allows any coaches you have not on summer contract to work elsewhere if need be), 2) This allows for my staff to meet after workouts and evaluate players throughout the summer (we normally meet one day a week for an "official" coaches meeting, but meet each day informally) and 3) This allows your team to begin bonding much earlier than August. I am a believer that 2-a-days and 3-a-days can be almost eliminated if players have been together to practice/bond throughout June and July. If you stagger workout times with your team throughout the summer and they are not all together, you cannot run any type of successful install and this sets you behind many teams that have been attending team camps, 7 on 7's and working as a team throughout the summer. While I am a believer in not overworking your team, I do feel that you should take advantage of whatever the practice/workout rules are in your state.

BUILDING A STAFF

In both of my head coaching jobs (and I'd say the norm for most places where success in football had not been very recent), I had very little say in who would be helping me as far as the hiring. Instead of getting rid of anyone that had been associated with the former staff, I was using them on my staff. I'd recommend to any coach if you have a chance to bring "your" guys in, that you do it, but this chapter will mainly be about taking what you have and making the most with it. As the time went on in both these jobs I was able to "phase" guys out by simply running things the way I saw fit and working hard to bring new assistants into my program and promote them as they earned experience.

I've learned in my time as a coach that you must get your staff to understand your WHY. If they understand what you believe in, and why you believe that way, and are on the same page, you may be on to something great. If you don't utilize your assistant coaches, you might as well have a staff of 1. I spend more time now with my assistants than I actually get to with my players. My goal is to make my assistant coaches an extension of me.

I have been blessed to work with some of the hardest working men in the business and during my time I've learned that these guys are extremely important to whatever you will accomplish as a head coach. The advice I am about to give is what I'd like to have done, and at times I have done many of these things, but I've also been very fortunate to have had some great guys already in place. I can only speak from my experience and the advice I've received from much smarter coaches than myself. All of them say to get your staff right as priority #1.

The first thing you have to do when coming into a "staff" already named for you, is to weed out the problems. I was not given the opportunity to hire anyone the first year I took over at one school and was only allowed to bring in 1 coach at another. So I had to find a way to create spots. In some states you can look to volunteers, but not in Arkansas and a few others. This creates a big problem as you can't just fire everyone on your staff. So what I typically do is make the first year a very "intense" year with lots of time and effort being spent. We work hard every year as a staff, but the first year is almost like a boot camp for my assistants. You cannot be fearful of moving coaches where you want them, even if it means demoting a coach that is very respected. You will be judged on how the team will do, and you must be comfortable with who you are working with and what position they will be coaching. In the following points I will show you what I do to get rid of coaches that do not fit with my program:

1. **The biggest fear I have had as a coach is to have a coach that is not loyal** to me (for good reason, I have only had to fire one coach so far in my career, and it was for this reason). To this end at times I have worked with coaches as to what I expect and allow to be said at each stop. This is also the first thing I look at when bringing in a coach as an assistant. I am not someone that cannot handle criticism or questioning, in the coach's meetings or in private. The quickest way to kill any chance you have of success for a team or a career, though, is to have someone in your program that cannot be trusted or is not loyal to you. I have been around some great head coaches, and I have been around some that were not as strong, but I have always been positive in public and in front of the team about each of them. I did this as an assistant and I expect my assistant coaches to do the same.

2. **Make the first season very tough and test the commitment of each coach on staff**. When I arrived at some schools I found there are a great number of coaches that want to move up, that feel much is "owed" to them, or that they have arrived or are on their way to being where they want to be, and they are not too interested in your program. I have no use for these guys and have always avoided hiring them. If they are already on your staff, quickly relegate them to jobs they can do, and have ears and eyes on them at all times. I have promoted others over them

in a heartbeat, and typically they would wash out of my program in a year. A lazy person will rub off on others, and a coach that is sloppy will also rub off on your players. You must make them understand the amount of effort and time required, and they will shape up or ship out. Usually, they ship out rather quickly. In one book I read they were referred to as "energy vampires".

3. **The next thing I look for in a coach is passion about their job**. Not every coach has to be a dynamic speaker or motivator on your staff, but all of them better love what they are doing. As with most staffs we put in extremely long hours. I am very careful as a family man to not "waste" time, but we meet 6-7 days a week. With programs like Hudl and the technology we have now, I allow my coaches to get their film study from home (but be careful to monitor this, usually you can do that by having a report due or asking them about something obvious in a coaches meeting. I have heard Hudl even allows you to monitor how much a coach/player has watched. I do this on purpose because it is another way to "weed out" coaches that are not passionate about what you are doing. We also require all coaches to be at most of our summer workouts, which run from 6:15AM-9:30AM for coaches. I want guys that want to be here enough that the work is not an issue. I was astounded at one school by the number of excuses from coaches as to why they couldn't make it. Just keep documentation on this and be sure to report it to your superintendent or superior at the end of the year overview. I was shocked at how many coaches in my first years knew when a workout was going on and would not come. This has to be addressed immediately as it will bleed into your staff.

4. Each year I do an **end of the year evaluation with every coach**. This is the best time to bring up issues that you have had with that individual. You should have already addressed most of these during the season as they happened. This allows each coach to know they work for you and will need to improve in certain areas if they would like to continue to do so. These meetings are my least favorite time of the year, as I typically get very close with my staff, but this is where a head coach must understand that they are the head of the program, and any problem they see must be addressed. The old saying is true, "If

you allow it; you accept it". Usually I hold these <u>2-3 weeks</u> after <u>the season so any anger on my or their part that may be in place</u> has had time to simmer and usually I can see clearer than right <u>after the season.</u> Again these meetings should not come as a shock to a coach if you have been communicating what you feel about them all season long.

The next <u>phase of coming into an already set group</u> of <u>coaches is to figure out who should be where on your staff.</u> I have already learned as a young coach that <u>work ethic is great as</u> is the ability to learn the game. I would rather have a coach that <u>will work his tail off and who</u> is fairly knowledgeable about the game than a very experienced coach that is not going to put in the type of effort that I demand from a coordinator. To me when I get to a school, I rank the importance of the level of each coach I need and fill from most important role on my staff to the least. <u>Great staffs have great coaches, and I'd rather have fewer quality coaches than many subpar coaches.</u> The reality of this situation is that many head coaches do not get to choose their staff, or if they do, at times they have to "settle for" some of their staff. While I understand that to have a great team, you must have great coaches at each spot on your staff, if you are walking into a situation where the program has not been successful, my guess is you will not have each coach at the level you would like, and the reality is you may have to deal with what staff is in place that you can work with.

In a perfect world here is how I rank my coaches. I've adjusted as needed, and each position is important, but if I was walking in today to a new situation, this is what I'd try to accomplish:

1. **Coordinator on side of the ball I will not be focused on**: This is your <u>right hand man.</u> He has <u>to be a guy that you can trust</u> to run the offense/defense with your philosophy and have the ability not only to create the system, but also be <u>in charge of other</u> <u>coaches that will be working underneath him.</u> If at all possible, this should be your <u>first hire</u> if you get to bring any coaches in.

2. **Offensive line coach**: To me this is the most overlooked position in high school football. There are very few programs I have ever

coached against that we did not look to exploit them up front. And if they were not well coached, we usually had great success as a defense. On the flip side, if a team beat us up front we rarely had a chance to beat them. To me this coach needs to be a guy who is a strong disciplinarian, and you need to hire him second if given a chance.

3. **Coordinator on side of the ball I will be focused on**: I have found this is a great spot to hire or move an "up-and-comer" type of younger coach that is very driven and energetic. I usually call one side of the ball, but have someone I am grooming at all times and this is the guy. I also will look to let him become the head JV coach. I have had a few good coordinators and if things go well, usually you will lose them to become a head coach somewhere else and this guy then takes over for whichever side of the ball he is on and you as the head coach can move to the other side of the ball and start grooming the next coordinator. If there is someone already on staff that I have liked, then I usually don't hire in this spot, just promote.

4. **QB Coach**: If you have the ability to have a great QB coach it is very important in today's game. Since many teams are going to the spread or offenses that rely heavily on a QB, this is an important job within your coaching staff. Many times your offensive coordinator can also assume this job, but I have found if you can hire a QB coach that has only that one job, usually you will get a lot more improvement from your QB's.

5. **Special Teams Coordinator**: This is usually a job for another younger coach, or a position coach that is very responsible. We take special teams very serious and want this coach to also feel this way. Most schools I have taken over were not very good in this area of the game, and it is an immediate improvement to place emphasis in this area at most high schools. A lot of times I am the special team's coordinator in my first season at a school, while I am grooming a younger coach to be ready to take the job.

6. **Linebacker coach**: Usually this is my defensive coordinator's position to coach, since I have never been able to have as large a staff as I'd like to have. This is the #1 spot to me with importance

to the defense, since they have to be working with both the defensive line and defensive backs. I am a big believer in playing intelligent (or at least as intelligent as you can) linebackers. We are very big on having them understand concepts and keys and they must be able to line all the other players.

7. **Offensive skill coach**: Depending on the offense you hope to run, this spot could fluctuate up or down on importance. Since I am a shotgun guy, we need to have a good receivers coach. Again, I am looking for a detail oriented guy. Doesn't have to have a ton of experience, but can learn the drills and teach them to our kids.

8. **Defensive skill coach**: Much like the offensive skill coach, this guy needs to be able to understand basic coverages and have several drill periods for the defensive backs. We usually want to keep our coverage simple and have our kids make plays. This is a great spot for a coach that has a lot of energy and is very optimistic as this spot can be tough to coach. We attempt to be very positive with our defensive backs, as we want them playing aggressive football trying to create turnovers and big plays for our defense.

9. **Defensive line coach**: Each spot is important, and I started as a defensive line coach so I have a special place for it in my heart. That being said, this spot needs to be coached up, but it is the most simple position to coach. Usually each team has 1-2 techniques and a few stunts and the defensive linemen rep the same drills over and over. I am looking for a coach here that will be able to motivate his linemen to play fast and hard and be a stickler for the details during drill work.

** **Strength Coach is a separate category for me. If you are able to bring in someone to run your strength program I'd highly recommend it.** Not all schools are blessed and able to do this, so I'd try to find someone who most represents you in this role. This coach is the next most vital coach on your staff if you hire or appoint one, so choose wisely as he will have a huge impact on your team's mentality. If you cannot hire a Strength Coach, I'd recommend that you do the job. This role is too important to leave to chance.

Usually each staff is different, but each staff must have not only position or coordinator roles, but also know what each coach will be expected to do within your "roles".

I have several "roles" for coaches that help to have a balanced staff. Usually I'd like to have (assuming just for this example that I have a staff of 8 coaches) 3-4 what I would call very positive energetic coaches that are very optimistic. I want every coach to be positive more often than not, but these guys need to be the ones that are very close to the kids and are the encouragers on the staff. Usually these are younger coaches. I want 2-3 coaches that are more x and o type guys that are very good at details and usually are my coordinators. This is usually a more experienced coach. I also need 2 coaches that are like drill sergeants. These guys can be old or young, but these are the coaches the players will fear and usually are the coaches I go to that will assist in handing out punishment.

What I have done as a coach is try to adapt my coaching style to where my staff needs a coach. Some staff's I have been with, I have needed energy and positive voices and that has been what I have done, and on another staff I have been the disciplinarian. You will find as a head coach at times you will need to be in each of these categories, but you need to be sure each role is filled on your staff. The balance may be different for you depending on your situation. Some schools may need more discipline, and some may need more x and o coaches. I have found that schools that have been struggling tend to need the enthusiasm and energy most, so I have looked for more coaches to fill those roles.

Creating "your" staff will take some time, but if you have a supportive administration (something to be sure to cover before you are hired) you may be able to get a list of what they are looking for in teachers and work any network you have at your access to get people to come in and interview. At a great school you may have more pull with the superintendent, but even at most schools, if you can dig up a coach that can teach math or science, they will at least get an interview with the school. This has been one way I have worked on bringing in coaches to the schools I have been associated with.

Do whatever is needed to help find great men of character to have in your program. You can teach a man of character how to coach football, but it is almost impossible to teach a coach how to have a great attitude and character. Bring in people you would want working with your son and teach them the game of football. If you work this way, you will be surprised how fast young coaches can learn the game.

X's and O's or Jack's and Joe's

This answer is very simple. Jack's and Joe's are what will win you football games. However, I am not a college coach, so I do not get to pick who decides to play football for me. So this chapter will cover 2 topics:

1) Making your Jack's and Joe's bigger and stronger and faster
2) Using your X's and O's to keep you in a game.

The game of football is not very complicated, unless we as coaches make it that way. Your job is to give your team the chance to score more than the other team. There are a ton of different philosophies, and it has been interesting for me to watch as a coach how other teams attempt to do this. Some try to simply out-score each opponent. This is fun to watch and can be effective with the right personnel and coaches. Some coaches stack their defense and attempt to run the ball and keep the score low. The objective for both is still the same, have more points than your opponent does.

Here is my philosophy. Whatever we try to do (and I tend to be more of a defensive minded guy) we will not beat ourselves. Too many times have I seen teams lose games without even making an opponent beat them. Especially teams that have not seen much success seem to have this issue. Teams I have taken over have not needed much of a change with x's and o's (although I do change to my system), but all of them have needed to learn how to not lose a game with issues in discipline, execution and basic football common sense. What I have always stressed from day one in regards to discipline on the field are the following: 1) No turnovers for our offense, 2) No "dumb" penalties, 3) Win special teams and 4) Win effort.

I've tried to read up on what great coaches do and most of them point to a few key points on the defensive side of the ball:

1. Be excellent in understanding of angles and responsibilities of your position.
2. Understand the situation of the game (not coaches only, but players).
3. Create turnovers any way you can.
4. Tackle as well as you physically can.
5. Know who on the other team can beat you and don't allow them to do so.

No turnovers on our offense is an impossible goal throughout the year, but we stress each day the responsibility we have as ball carriers and QB's to take care of the football. This means in practice there are consequences for fumbles or INT's thrown. This doesn't mean we don't look to make plays. We just know how to be smart with the ball. As a coach this also affects your play selection (whether it be you as the Head Coach or Offensive Coordinator). You have to be willing to punt the ball. 3rd and longs can be a great opportunity to challenge a defense, but are also a place where lots of bad things happen to offenses, so be careful on what you plan to call.

No "dumb" penalties. We define these as before or after the play penalties or penalties that are done for selfish reasons (cheap shot behind the play, etc...). These are something I am still working on with my teams after year 2,3 and 4 as they are tough to gain. We have a goal of no procedure penalties or "Unsportsmanlike" penalties. I tried to include personal fouls, but facemasks and hits right on the sideline are too tough to police, so we made it only unsportsmanlike (talking, cheap shots, etc...). Unless you are simply much better than your opponent, usually you will lose the game if you lose in the penalty or turnover battle.

Win the special teams. It is odd to me that with so many great coaches I have coached against or watched coach, this is still a very neglected part of the game. Each year I have coached we have always had at least 2-3 kicks blocked and a return for a touchdown. As of now (knock on wood) I have never given up a return for a touchdown and only had 2 kicks blocked. This is an area that you don't want to spend a crazy amount of time on during the week and take away from your offense/defense, but you must find a way to create big plays and never give them up. Some of the things we do on special teams:

Kickoff: We set our kickoff with the ability to move the ball all over the field and call from the sideline as to how the team is aligned. Basically, we do colors for the 3 sectors of the field from left to right and numbers for how deep we want the ball kicked. This does require your kicker to have time to practice (usually we do a 10 minute pre-practice with kickers/holders/punters/snappers/returners each day). This allows for you to kick away from the other team's best players. We never want to give up a big return and will sacrifice allowing the team to take the ball from their 35 yard line if need be. I am also a huge believer in the pooch kick and attempting to get the ball back and steal possessions if the opportunity arises. If you can kick it to the end zone do it every time, but I have not been blessed with that opportunity.

KOR: We normally scout where the other team's kicks have landed each week and base our alignment and return off of that. Several times I have moved my two best kids up on a return because the other kicker has been putting it short. We always have a simple return for deep kicks. The front line form a wall on either sideline (depending on call), and we kick out contain guy to that direction. The rules in the back are very simple: a) If the deep man catches, we fake reverse away from the wall, b) If wall side returner catches, we give reverse to deep man and c) If returner away from wall catches ball, both other returners block middle to allow him to get to the wall. We have also done returns where we only block one side of the field when teams directional kick. This to us is a huge opportunity to make a big play and we work one schemed return a week along with our wall return.

Punt: Must be sound. 100's of ways to do this. We have gone to kicking from our base formation, due to having a hard time finding snappers. We will try to have our QB punt the ball if at all possible as it makes teams much more nervous about setting up a return.

Punt Block/Return: I have always attempted to watch film on an opponent and see where the weakness is. If you cannot spot a weakness, don't waste a lot of time on return/block, but if you do find one you have to be aggressive in going after it. Using twists or simply outnumbering your opponent will give you a great chance to block a punt. One word of caution. Be sure to coach how you want the kick blocked, and pick wisely in who you are sending after a kick because a roughing-the-kicker call can kill you.

XP/FG: You must find a kicker that can be great on XP's. How many games do we see lost by 1 point? Too many in my opinion. We work the snap and hold every day. Our kicker will get 5 minutes a day on XP's and then we will look at FG's and Kickoffs. We choose to do the swinging gate on all XP's because I was surprised how many teams were not prepared for it. It is very simple to put in early in the year, and it helped us go 6-6 on 2 pt. conversions just this past season. One quick tip on the gate: Make sure your snapper is eligible. He is almost never covered!

XP/FG Block: We don't spend a ton of time on this. Basically we overload a side off the edge and have 2-3 committed to rushing the middle and jumping. Be sure you show your team all the eligible receivers, and keep men to account for them. One thing we do go over each Thursday in pre-game is "sell-out" block. In a game we have to stop this FG/XP to win or tie we want to know what we will do. Again, we use the same idea (to overload a side and middle area), and bring more than they can block.

This sounds like a lot, but if it is put in slowly during the preseason, all that will be needed is a few minor scheme changes week to week. We typically practice specialty (kicking/holding/snapping/returning) for 10 minutes each day (other players are working XP/FG block or running lanes for kickoff during this time), and we work special teams 20 minutes on Monday, 15 on Tuesday, 10 on Wednesday and go over each in walk through on Thursday.

All this will not matter if you do not get effort out of your kids. I have done a lot of things to encourage great effort.
1. We grade each player as coaches (1 point for effort, 1 point for technique) and make notes on HUDL so players can see where they lost points. As a head coach I am much more interested in effort than technique (as we can coach them up throughout the year). At the high school level if you are not grading your players they will not improve. This is a must in watching film and teaches your assistant coaches how you expect them to grade film. All

grades get turned in to me by the position coach. If a player has multiple loaf's we warn him (usually this happens to a younger player on the first time graded), the second time he will do some "extra work" after practice and the third time he will be on the bench. Loafs cannot be accepted by any coach that wants a successful program. It was a hard thing to do for me as a younger coach, but learning that max effort is something you must have, and even sacrificing talent at times if it is not there.

2. We also even give scout team player of the week to a non-starter to encourage great effort throughout the week in practice. This player gets to lead the team out through the run-through on game night. He also gets a player-of-the-week shirt. (Kids will do almost anything for a shirt). We want each kid on the team to know their effort is noticed and expected each practice. I have also lined the boys up for conditioning after a great practice and called off conditioning as a reward for their effort. (Usually I hadn't planned on running anyway, but they didn't have to know that part).

3. Early in the season we will dedicate 5-10 minutes a practice for a pursuit drill. We have everyone in a group (including non-defensive players), and teach them the correct angle and then run them through the drill 10-15 times at a very fast pace, and do not allow loaf's. We usually add a turnover session where they are taught where to go should we get a turnover and want to return it. Very simple drill, but the point gets through quickly (especially the first time you make them re-do it because someone in the group was not giving max effort).

X's and O's

There are a ton of really great coaches out there, but I have found that many rely completely on their "system" and don't do a great job of game-planning for an opponent. I am a believer in being good at what you do, but we also need to make sure we are prepared to adjust to what we will see. Tweaking the offense and defense with simple adjustments to your system are a must if you want to compete with teams that may have better talent than you do. We spend Sunday evenings after we have done our own film and work on how to attack an opponent. I have not won every game, but most of the time I feel we have given our kids the best chance to win by doing the following each week.

Below is my philosophy on how to make sure you maximize your defense and use your talent to take away the opponents best players. If you could sum up what we attempt to do on defense each week it is that – Make the other team beat us with their #3, #4 or #5 weapons.

DEFENSIVELY

Details matter - Remember the story of the oranges from the previous chapter. Someone on your defensive staff (and that someone may be you) must hunt down all the details. I'm not just talking about the ones Hudl gives you, but all the details. Once you have them you have to figure out the **WHY** of the opposite coach. Then you have to figure out how to get out all the stuff that doesn't matter so you don't overload your kids.

1. We breakdown all information on an opponent as a coaching staff. This includes formations, down-distance tendencies, play after turnover, play after big play, hash plays, pass play targets (who and where), favorite side to run the ball to (or if they switch offensive linemen), gimmick plays and more. Most coaches do this. Where I think I have been good is to not overload my kids with "stuff" they don't need. Here is what we expect of our kids:

    A. Know top 5 formations and what plays they run out of them

    B. Percentage run or pass out of formation or down and distance

    C. Know any "automatics" – Example: Team runs 100% in this formation or throws 100%

    D. 3 Favorite routes – Our DB's are great if we know what the combos are or where they like to go with the ball. Most high school QB's and coaches run plays to get the ball to a certain player, and we want to take that away and make someone else beat us. We can also jump routes with LB's and Corners if they know what is being run.

E.   KEYS: This is #1 for LB's. We typically spend most of our time teaching this. It needs to be 90% right or more – For example: Guards vs. Wing-T, or FB in "I" or Offensive Line in Spread. They also need to know where their eyes go on passes, and we never cover a zone, but a man in our zone.

F.   Any checks we have to formations

G.   Who are the studs from the other team. You'd be surprised how many high school kids were a little freaked out that our kids were calling out their names and pointing to them when they lined up and telling routes or what to watch. It is always a mental game and any advantage we can get is great.

2.   The rest of our defense is based on learning this information (we spend most of Monday at a slower pace). We will grill the boys on keys before each play Tuesday and on some plays Wednesday as we start running more plays at them.

3.   One other thing I have done well is to have 2 groups prepared. On teams where I have had the numbers we have done 2 defenses and offenses going at the same time with JV coaches working with #2's. The part of this we don't like is some of your rotation guys don't get the best reps, but I feel it is worth it as they are getting way more reps each week.

4.   Make sure your individual time is drills that matter. Every coach has 100's of drills (or just a simple google search will bring them up), but what great coaches do is use drills that matter. We spend 5-10 minutes a day on tackling, 5 on turnovers, 5 on agility type drills and the other 10-15 is to work on something we will use in a game. If you will be playing man-to-man all week, don't work zone, if you will have your defensive linemen head up and stunting don't work "3" or "1" techniques, etc...

**There are not many things in life that will upset me more than when I see a position group not using their entire time period working on individual drills that fit. We do a drill book to help our younger coaches, but I do not want to see groups get done early or working on drills that will never translate to a game. **

5. <u>Place an emphasis on defense in how you talk to the team</u>. I have found that teams where kids want to play defense tend to be the most successful teams. Most boys grow up dreaming of playing offense and that has trickled into the high school level as many youth coaches play their best players on offense. Especially if you are a Head Coach that runs the offense, you must be involved with the defense and know what is going on, so the kids realize you understand what they are doing. Whether you choose to put your best on defense is up to you, but make them feel as if they are the most important part of your team. The old saying is true, "Offense wins games, defense wins championships", and even if you are stacking your offense, your defense has to believe in themselves.

OFFENSIVELY

One thing I learned quickly as an offensive play caller is to not do anything "extra" until you are solid with your base offense. Many offenses we watch may run 100's of plays, but struggle with simple things that I believe all offenses must be good at: 1) Blocking all fronts/stunts, 2) Handling the blitz in run and pass game and 3) Not hurting self (dropped passes, penalties, missed routes). To me we spend most of our practices going over the basics and maybe 5-10 minutes with "gameplan" plays or adjustments that we have put in for that week. We usually take out way more of our offense in practice than we will "gameplan" for by putting in.

Our typical in-season practice will feature 10 minutes on a circuit with REC/QB working routes at very high tempo, RB working ball drills (catch, cut, fumble drill) and Offensive line working ladder. We then move to 15 minutes of individual work, 10-15 of "group" and 15 of "team". One thing we have learned is working at a high pace through group/team and circuit allows you way more reps. We will slow down our pace some in individual depending on the drill we are putting in and at times the last 5 minutes of that may be an "install" time for position coaches. Usually all our install for any new formation or play we will run comes in on Monday, and we will get 4-5 reps in team with each one.

We make any changes to our play-calling chart on Monday by taking out plays we don't feel are a good fit for the team we are going against based off their personnel or defensive style. Like most teams we have routes against cover 2 or cover 3 or man-to-man. If a team plays all 3 defenses we will leave our plays as that will be an adjustment during a game.

Here is what I instruct our coaches to watch while watching film of an opponent:

1. Personnel: We want to see who will be a great matchup for us, and who will be a problem for our team. This is an easier job, because we want to only game-plan for a kid if it is obvious to all. I assign this job to typically a junior high coach.

2. Down-Distance changes: This is where we want to see how aggressive the other coach is. If it is 3rd and long or 2nd and long will he come after us? Does he have a favorite coverage in obvious passing situations? What is their "normal" defense on 1st and 10? This won't completely change my playcalling, but it may give me an edge. I assign this job to a position coach.

3. Hash defense: I think this is the most underused part of scouting by most people. When I see a defensive coordinator that stays "balanced" to the boundary and wide side of the field, we will go wide side every time. You can also see that many defensive coordinators love to bring pressure off the short side, and if that is the case, we love the short passing or screen game into the boundary. I assign this to my QB coach.

4. 4th quarter or last minute defense: To me you can find out what is really going on inside the head of a DC by watching how he calls a defense in the 4th quarter. When it comes down to it, what is he going to do? Will he bring pressure or play conservative? We also love to see what they do in the 2-minute defense or nickel look. I assign this to a position coach.

Goal Line Defense: What will the defense do inside the 10-yard line? The 20-yard line? This is an area of the field you must excel at if you want to win games. Most defenses are pretty simple and do the same type of defense in the red zone, but it definitely changes from what they call in the middle of the field. You could also call this 4th and short defense. I assign this to a position coach, usually my Offensive Line Coach.

Mistakes I've Made

This chapter will be lots of little stories of things I've done that I wish I could go back and tell myself to change. Hopefully one or two may be able to help you avoid the same issues.

First mistake — What you allow to slide, you accept. As a coach I've seen it several times that I simply get tired or do not recognize something small and don't address it. Whatever you think is important must be upheld or it really isn't important. I've tried to have as few rules as possible, but those I have, I try to enforce.

Example— My second season as a head coach I had several very good players that were always "hurt" during the week, but were good to go on Thursday walk through practice and in Friday games were out there crushing people. One of my assistants even coined the phrase "Miracle Thursdays". As the season went on we had more and more injured players.

The fix — We now have every player dress out even if they are non-contact players. Everyone has a helmet and whatever gear they are allowed to wear. If they are actually injured they are in the ice bath or away from the field. Those who are injured somewhat are with their position groups with helmet and practice jersey. I've even had some with that and a boot on a foot. I explain to them that I don't expect them to violate a doctor's order, but we will do everything we can to be a part of the team and not a distraction.

Second mistake — If we won the game I did a great job as a coach, and if we lost I did a terrible job. I've had the pleasure of going 10-2 recently with our first ever conference championship and I've also had the excruciating pain of going 0-10.

69

Example — My second season I was very fortunate to have some great players. We made the playoffs in 4A for the first time in school history. We hosted our first playoff game in 20-years and in general had a great season. While I did some things well, I was allowing our culture to become all about winning and sacrificing discipline. The next season we went 3-8 with an even more talented group.

The fix — I started holding myself to a much higher standard than some lousy scoreboard on a Friday night. Am I teaching these boys how to become great young men? Am I holding them accountable? Am I teaching my assistants what I expect from them? If I can answer these things with a yes, then I honestly don't care about the scoreboard. The irony is we are actually winning more now than ever before, and I don't obsess over winning at all cost.

Third mistake — Thinking everyone in my program cares as much about football as I do. I learned very quickly that someone with the desire to be a head coach has much more football obsession than your average football player and even your average football assistant. This does not make them bad people or people that don't care. It just makes them normal people.

Example — I can vividly remember getting frustrated early on in my career when I'd have a player that hadn't read his scouting report, watched his film and done all the other things I required them to do by Monday. I'd just finished jumping all over him (in front of the team) when I was informed by an assistant in private that he had to work all weekend because his dad had lost his job and he was now paying bills for the family. Talk about a humbling moment.

The fix — First I spend a lot more time getting to know the situation of my players. I also pick 2-3 guys that are obsessed with football on each side of the ball and give them much more responsibility of making adjustments during a game than the "average" player. Most teams have 3-4 guys that are film junkies and we give these guys roles within the team — For example, we try to have one safety (ability doesn't matter as much as long as he is good enough to be on the field) call the coverage adjusts and we do the same at linebacker and offensive line. The only position I must have a guy who loves the game as much as me is the QB position.

CONCLUSION

I do not claim to have very many answers to how to be a great coach and I honestly feel there are tons of great examples of guys that do it their own way. This book was just my way of sharing things I wish I had known when I'd been thrown my first head football position at the age of 28. I've made (and continue to make) lots of mistakes as a coach, but through my time I've learned more and more about the awesome responsibility a coach has to his players.

Be aware that your words carry a lot of weight, and you are being watched by lots of eyes. I've had players come back and share stories of some of the things I've said that they still remember, and I didn't even realize at the time that what I was saying or doing even really mattered to them. The Bible says it so much better than I can in Proverbs 18:4, "A person's words can be life giving water; words of true wisdom are as refreshing as a babbling brook." I've coached long enough that some of my former players are no longer with us, and I wish I could go back and say something to them that may have changed the trajectory of their life. Be an encourager in a world that wants to beat down young men.

Don't let those who want to criticize you run you out of the game either. Lots of people want your job after a big win, but many don't know or want all the hours and weeks that lead up to those moments. As Teddy Roosevelt said "It is not the critic who counts; not the man who points out how the strong man stumbles, or where the doer of deeds could have done them better. The credit belongs to the man who is actually in the arena, whose face is marred by dust and sweat and blood; who strives valiantly; who errs, who comes short again and again, because there is no effort without error and shortcoming; but who does actually strive to do the deeds; who knows great enthusiasms, the great devotions; who spends himself in a worthy cause; who at the best knows in the end the triumph of high achievement, and who at the worst, if he fails, at least fails while daring greatly, so that his place shall never be with those cold and timid souls who neither know victory nor defeat".

I've been the "Coach of the Year" a few times by different organizations and I've been 0-10. Stay true to who you are and your core beliefs through both times, and you will show the people that matter the most to you that you are a man of character. If you change with your circumstances then you are not a man of character, those who succeed in life live by the same standards through the "wins" and "losses" on the scoreboards.

ABOUT THE AUTHOR

Kenny Simpson is the Head Football Coach at Southside High School, a 4A school in Arkansas. He holds school records in every major category including: wins, points scored, points allowed. In 2017 Simpson was selected as a Finalist for the Hooten's Coach of the Year in 4A. The 10 wins in 2017 were also a record at Southside. Simpson was also selected as the 4A-2 Coach of the Year in 2017. In 2016, he was selected as the All-Star Nominee for the 4A-2. Southside had never won more than three games in a season before his arrival. They have now posted several consecutive playoff births'.

Simpson oversaw a field turf project, a fieldhouse expansion project, a new press box, and the acquisition of a digital scoreboard. He has also fundraised for over $35,000 in weight room equipment and received two grants for equipment.

Before coaching at Southside, Simpson was the Head Coach at Alabama Christian Academy in Montgomery, Alabama. During his tenure there, Simpson took a team that had been 4-16 the previous seasons and led them to an 18-16 record. For his successes, Simpson was named Montgomery Advertiser's All-Metro Coach of the Year as well as 4A Region 2 Coach of the Year. Under his direction, ACA's offenses in 2009 and 2010 each set school records for points scored in a season as well as leading the conference both years in points scored. Simpson began his coaching career at Madison Academy, in Huntsville, Alabama. He graduated from Harding University in 2003. He is married to Jamey and has three children: Avery, Braden, and Bennett. The couple has been married since 2001 after meeting at Harding University.

Made in the USA
Middletown, DE
26 May 2021